EXALTATION IN
CADMIUM RED

first poets series 11

Canada Council   Conseil des Arts
for the Arts   du Canada

ONTARIO ARTS COUNCIL
CONSEIL DES ARTS DE L'ONTARIO

Guernica Editions Inc. acknowledges the support of
the Canada Council for the Arts and the Ontario Arts Council.
The Ontario Arts Council is an agency of the Government of Ontario.

Exaltation

in

Cadmium Red

Sonia Di Placido

Sonia Di Placido

GUERNICA

TORONTO – BUFFALO – BERKELEY – LANCASTER (U.K.) 2012

First edition.
Printed in Canada.

Michael Mirolla, editor
Elana Wolff, poetry editor
Guernica Editions Inc.
P.O. Box 117, Station P, Toronto (ON), Canada M5S 2S6
2250 Military Road, Tonawanda, N.Y. 14150-6000 U.S.A.

Distributors:
University of Toronto Press Distribution,
5201 Dufferin Street, Toronto (ON), Canada M3H 5T8
Gazelle Book Services, White Cross Mills, High
Town, Lancaster LA1 4XS U.K.
Small Press Distribution, 1341 Seventh St.,
Berkeley, CA 94710-1409 U.S.A.

Legal Deposit – Third Quarter
Library of Congress Catalog Card Number: 2012938354

Library and Archives Canada Cataloguing in Publication

Di Placido, Sonia
Exaltation in cadmium red / Sonia Di Placido.

(First poets series ; 11)
Poems.
Issued also in electronic format.
ISBN 978-1-55071-618-4

I. Title. II. Series: First poets series (Toronto, Ont.) ; 11

PS8607.I685E93 2012   C811'.6   C2012-902897-5

Contents

for Mother

Hold me close, friend –
What is our worth?

Dear Gary,

thankyou so much for
your support and
what you've done for
Madison — we've moved
to a whole new level.

With admiration,

love Sarin

Perditi, bimba
di pasta e burro,
rosso-buccia di
mela, torna sempre
di piú di farina,
di polpa, gli
occhi, il cuore
che si sciolgano
informi,
          ritorna qui
in bocca alla tua
mamma.

– Elisa Biagini, *Perditi, bimba*

Lose yourself, child
of dough and butter,
red-peel of an
apple, return more and
more flour,
flesh, your
eyes, your heart
melting
formless,
          return here
to your mother's
mouth.

– Elisa Biagini, from *Lose Yourself, Child*

The Rigour

The rigorous labour of love
keeps no day or night.
Only the blood-filled intensity of
doing and done.
A being, brought and bought.
Do you know what it is?

The Rigour,
it dances before the
rigor mortis – the welcome
after persistent clenching
of muscle and flesh
gone stiff.

Tasting phrases,
quipping words,
Multiplying outward.
It knows only
patterns of passion,
craving itself line by line.

Occupy This Room

Occupy these words – willful
regimented type
without remission.
Occupy this wire,
the ink ribbon,
tardy electric phrases,
archaic instruments.
Occupy the [w]rite of metal
clinch, orchestrate the space.
Occupy Corpus Christi
in reverse.
Occupy the anima,
this room.

Now You Know

what you have to do. Next time. It isn't about jumping fences anymore, like when the baseballs flew into Mrs. Raconelli's yard. The Oh-shit task of the next tactic – making the balls less difficult to get to when they disappear from the common ground. It's the combustion point of when to say good-bye to the thing you think you love, how it's done. The scar you're going to make on the right shin as you scrape. The wobbly metal frame you don't notice as your knickers tear, the German Shepherd on the far left lawn, the terror of being more awake. Better pitch. Better aim, South Paw, soft paw.

Pew

Kneeling
in cathedrals
where the bells toll each hour –
St. James, St. Andrew, St. Michael,
Anglican, Baptist, Catholic.

Heads bowed in humble faith
listening for the beatitudes.
This is what the angels do, so it is written.
The statues watch, wait for us to somehow
fly out of these domed roofs.

Breathe as if you've been moving.
Say Pietà, Say it
fresh for a moment of peace.
Reel the idleness out,
in awe.

Make of yourself a stone statue
with a pretense to weep, stay mock-still.
Instead, you lean on the pew,
cross your legs to inspect
the above –
plaster ornaments, raw paintings that gleam.

The Words

We have watched you, felt you flick the pages, the reprints. We have come with you on this trip where remnants of letters keep falling from the voice you are trying to keep. Some days we are laughing at you. Most days we don't dare. What you choose from us is never boring, yet we feel, and often, we're a horrid contemplation. Tampered with again, again. Tricked, erased, and muddled, till we feel cut in the flesh of each letter. You call it fumbling badly. All we can do is remind you we're not apathetic; this is not a joke. Not just writable spin over page where dregs stay pregnant with passage. We spoke. We speak.

Imaginings

I could have announced to the world
on this night
what I've seen of you,

in the exact shape of my longing –
the papers, the paint, the tool thrown
and thrust about you. The centuries-old ink

that stains your fingers, the garb of your
tattered cloak, the messages you sing.
But how to demonstrate? That's

your task not mine, though I'd like to mimic.
How plain that would be.
In the rooms we know – these storytelling lounges –

there are angels that fall,
come down,
then linger with such precision to position.

I couldn't have guessed without really
seeing into kaleidoscopes, microscopes, the looking
glasses that give us miniature imaginings to laugh at.

The artist constructing, taking his earthen
canvas to task on wings.
I could say you've found your

below, the work of bellowing song from shoe to
stone. All the libations to consider, such malleability.
Just enough skin for this world.

Pilgrim

If there is no God,
Not everything is permitted to man.
He is still his brother's keeper
And he is not permitted to sadden his brother,
By saying that there is no God.

— Czeslaw Milosz

A pilgrim is sleeping,
waiting for the wake-up call.
The dial tone expired,
his neurons shorted out.
Captivated by his own coma,
defunct like copper,
he is incapable of a charge.

Tell Me

where the dead children live. It's my duty to visit them
with poetry and gifts – doves for purity, jam for sweetness,
drums to dissipate, dream away demons. Shoes to stomp out
lonely feelings, paint to swell their senses. Marbles for each child
to see our world, so they may visit whenever they choose.

Big Things

I'm dying to tell you about big things,
great things that we find with our fingers.
But I have lost the will to use
my fingers, so you'll have to settle for
little charms – the ladybug
that flew onto my right ring finger one afternoon,
the summer I sat in David Crombie Park,
              alone.
The steel sauce bowl at Windmill Line
that welcomed all four of my licked fingers,
after each of three fancy dinners
for a group of poets,
              once friends.
Most importantly, the knife I used
to try and cut a finger when I started to
know I was not well-loved by the person
who talked about all the great big things –
those not real between us.
              No, none of that.
Only small selfish desires the fingers ache for –
such things as the clever writing of big words.

Ghost Dialogue

Let's be friends you and I, your pain is mine
— Elizabeth Smart

I must have known you were here,
tucked away in a corner of the nest. Your mouth,
your words, your living soul, its itch.
I sought your station. Somehow, I pictured St. George.

There you were crooning from the third bookshelf –
my mother's oak. There you were limbering, gushing,
yelling to jump off the panel, custom-made by dad,
onto the hardwood floor beside the Belgian rug –

an antique. I recall the empty afternoons, snuggled
into the side of the sofa, flipping through your pages.
The 1955 edition. The living room pouring in rays,
sunlight filling a peaceful pasture, your blackened

paperback. I, an object of taxidermy, ornamental,
opened by your magic. Longing for a friend.
I dabbled into the blood of what you wrote.
I carry it, reaching for the pain.

Prelude

Let the words
melt into lava
or larvae,

destroy

them/then

create

them/then

destroy

them/then

create

then/them.

Destroy

them then.

Diabla

I've seen her
splashing murky waters,
calling up frogs and toads,
waiting to be kissed.

They crave her voice –
her princess mimics the ribbits,
woos the fresh lake water –
wet and rough in spring.

I've caught her skinny-dipping,
summer dashing,
climbing pines.
Skipping over rocks

and grassy sheaves.
Climbing high, I find her
finger-licking, tripping dizzy.
Living mean.

The Craft

I'm heading west.
Getting really good at this.

The process, in keeping with its fluidity,
is a monotony more constant than driving straight ahead.

There is always this middle view of a flat prairie horizon,
eternity to the eye.

Until you reach an edge,
that glorious view.

The Aftermath

brings dark
whispers,
howling diction,
perverse jewelry,
removal of shoes,
a sore scapula,
mascara melted
into skin.

The heroine
of this dirty chivalry
rests till noon, wakens,
ripped at dusk.

The Mark of A Bad Lover

I do not wish to know
the mark of a bad lover,
but I've known myself,
and this is how I know

you, who have hunted like Jack,
leading the cult
of the pig –
the one that kills his seed.

The Hangman Favours Apollo

I should have heeded the warnings
of Medusa: that in her wrath,
she not only turns men to stone,
but also poisons love. Not even Zeus
can outdo her destructions. Perhaps
then, the cards would have worked in
my favour. But when dealing with Apollo,
who hangs between his father, Zeus,

and Hera – that vindictive temptress –
failure is his fate. He hides his love
inside the clouds, staking airs
of greatness. Seeks a Dionysian girl.
Little does he know
she'll transform into a nemesis.
Sorceress, Olympia,
seductress of reptilian things.

End of the Affair

I saw Venice
drowned in screams,

Casanova dancing up the shores,
jilting waves,

saluting shame.
Love-dormant gondolas

waiting for a salt-water release.
San Marco's pigeons

mourning the non-existent trees.
Air collapses

when romance gets trapped.
I found Venice

aimless for her dreams.

Tomorrow

We'll waltz
in vineyards,
drunk on audacity,
spewing, loose.

Our mouths will chew
Italian wheat,
language will tickle
both tongues.

I could love you again
in my silly stupor,
of blindness.
My stubborn mould.

Holy One at the Gate

Panhandler, had I food and fortune enough,
I would redeem it for you.
You would have my dwelling
in this narrow laneway too –

the remainder of love and longing.
But there is no freedom in it.
Only your scarecrow frame,
behind my earthier one.

The Old World

The tilled fields remain. Each season pliant and green, wild with vines and grapes. Sea in the distance. Grasshoppers and thistles, pebbles and stones choking the air. Memory of a donkey wagon passing. The peasants faded and worn. Olive groves. Distances splitting east and west, purples and blues, row on row, the setting sun a silence, aglow. Stones of abandoned homes. Vesuvius of a maddened mother, her grasp, the pulse of time, all glory tanked. Strips of terrain reminiscent of lovers forced to part at dusk. Wells keeping their secrets. Hot malicious days. Nature's pillars crumbling – unseen, back-beaten. End of two into one.

Skins Over Pompeii

You write your skin over Pompeii,
narrow the focus on stone-remains
that lift from embers, lava and ash.

What else is there?
The restless search, this capsule
we both know, the ancient city we share.

You were hammered, sodden, drowned.
I am here, alive. It's thirty-five
years since your murder,

my birth. We meet, our hurting skins,
a poem not yet proof:
I'm the new flesh of your land.

Tongue, skin, bone, breath into gesture.
Our absolute stations of dance with words
mimicking catacombed griefs.

I've finger-skinned their surfaces,
come to find you here.
I know this place, my blunt tattoo –

once juice, now skin over burnt clay.

Soothsayer

I have waved the worn wooden
wand before you,

demonstrated lush networks of
fortune that have then been made lost.

I have brought words shepherded
from valleys, woven from wool,

tapestries plaited in vegetable
dye, grains in grassy hues.

Wise texts built again and again,
through eons and star-speckled epochs.

Minor prophets shaping textiles
out of particle dust.

Baby Denim

You will live long enough to wear
me out on a Friday night.
Torn threads, oil stains,
frayed cotton
fringes.
Having outlived six years of wash,
blue friends, blue accidents,
blue flowers are my learning.

Blue Flowering

Sleep with me under pines,
slap ebony on these breasts,
breathe toxins into northern nights.
Blow over me with wind and
whistle naked blooming truths.
Uncurl our creature into design,
Push your flesh to blue in mine.

Cadmium Red

I tried to share it with you:
how to take apart the toxic words –
the red strokes that obliterate.

But you'll never get it; unless you come
to see your red splatter as a habit in its ugly
vastness – a canvas caught, distraught.

How ferociousness must stay within
the bounds of some aperture or design,
however abstract on its blank canvas.

This is part of the secret when working
in cadmium red. Knowing the first brush
stroke, feeling out when to stop the colour

from overbearing the white space. Knowing
how much pigment is too much for one piece.
How to ease out the measure between paint

and brush with the grip of your fingers. Same
as the dip of a feather tip writing in blood.
The object becomes subtle, sacred, and sleek.

It was fun for a while – making bold red
splotches and strokes of desire. The thick
smell of oil perverse till dried. I began to see

the red tragedy reflected through your eyes –
what had not been imbued.
The lack of skill for containing such

wanton passion, intricate pleasure.
What is most required when releasing
the awe of a cadmium romance.

Death Fruit

I watched it all blow away, every stone
millimetre of statue, my lust forever
intensified by Mussolini's fascist charms.
Same as the madness of the village chinks
cackling obscenities at the Germans
who seized each of our towns; the children

understand nothing; their skins flapping for
salt-water breeze, rushing into the charcoal
atmosphere. That summer was like a seaside
dream before they blasted the Gelato house.
We thought death was beyond us, but the crucial
moment flared and the mortal in me screamed

at two boys hiding in ruin, *Scappa! Scappa!
Su! Dai!* Run! Run! Come on! Up and Away!
Let's go! The younger one yelling and pointing:
Bomba! Distant screams are heard. We run
two kilometres to the tracks. I'm sorry about the
missing luggage, the few clothes. I'm panting,

ecstatic. I want to catch you. Fumble, falling
slowly in the hot excitement of words. You,
an anxious anomaly, pace the furthest corner
of the station. The two boys scurry ahead.
I wore my silk dress that day – the one from
Alfredo, our tailor. When our eyes met

and you looked me over, covered in soot,
you yelled: "We could've been here before
the collapse began!" I took time to prepare
my best dress and luggage when the blitz came
unexpected, hours early. Despite the train blast
and the loss of our gold, that's how I forever

know you love me. I knew when they pelted
you seconds after I spoke, it was the last song
from your mouth. How long I stood cowering
over you. Deliberate. Shredded silk and coal. The
boys too scared to return. I cower still over what
survived. The kitchen floor is marbled purple dust.

Excerpt From A Cowgirl Diary

Twenty-five yards to the schoolhouse; his boots crunch
wild flowers, chirping grasshoppers, count the uphill climb.
I strike a match that burns our gaze to the acetate paper,
my books. He glances at the wooden fence, leather hat low
on his head, leans in for a squint, frames a girl on either side,
chews tobacco. Silent stares. Rebel Lips. Any girl would want
to abandon here. I reach for the breeze, draw each orifice.
All that provides for the bumblebee.

Zuppolone

A village in eroded mountains connected to the Alps. Donkey wagons making passage, peasants ploughing fields. Picking and counting their scores. Competitive bouts with wine and bread each day.

A large man walks among the vineyards, apple orchards, olive groves. Clay jug on his back – Molise wine. Zuppolone, he's called, the man who can drink more than anyone else in the village. The one who takes his wine with bread each morning. A jug as large as a demijohn.

He makes his salutations to God, *suo corpo* – Christ-like, becoming a legacy. Elated as the sun bears down his back.

The clan of Zuppolone from Colle Bove, Torrella del Sannio, Molise. A family of winos, even now, with cantinas brimming over in the hamlet miles from town. Across an ocean, in Canada, we drink this nectar like a juice that makes our bones scarlet and keeps our spirits light.

Aria for Evita

Her mouth of hot air, *La Boca*, embraced me thrice:
I danced with her missing pieces in Buenos Aires
the decade her body-snatchers ransomed

the neighbourhood for her stolen, ailing body.
Evita of folktale fancy and a nationalistic stint.
The people screamed, she shorted out, and yet

was welcomed again and again. Churches crowned her,
crimson worship churned the musty, incensed air.
I found her hiding under a table, preparing soon

to lift. The toss of celebration great. Sweat streamed
down from bodies, dripping on plates.
"I am a heated Argentine Queen pillaged for a dream,"

she told me. We met again in the garden and slept,
the outdoor oven crackling in the hemispheric glare.
A fiesta *por l'estragnero*. Loud incongruent messages

in Italian/Argentine. Maté, maté, maté,
scent of lemons, alcohol fix. A final family fracas
where my grand old uncles lost their grip.

How I'd Like to Die

I want us to be friends –
patient for each other, playing poker
not bridge, bluffing by early dusk.

I'd like to suffer the moment,
and age, like a fine
Sangiovese staining my marrow;

move through days at eighty, ninety,
hands quivering, bones
turning to glass preparing to shatter.

I'd like to be reminded of the tick-tock
coming close,
each internal-step a stare-down match –

the way a bull sees red,
its horns like whips and arrows,
whispers, sighs. I want to die

equipped for the jolt, a steadfast grip
on the scythe, my fingers unafraid of slipping.
Whether the head is sliced

or severed, let the sweep be clean.
I *don't* want to awaken in the dis/enchanted
wood. I want us to be friends, and patient,

shameless, too, behind the bluff;
to claim a fierce respect for mystery –
this is how I want to live.

Trans-Nation

We're tossed among bone-cemented joints of city streets, towers of impeccable glass. Sky-scraped. We crack as we build, but are not above progress. If every child stinks with the sewage of politics and governing bile, we can clean them. Make them dance. Replant forests, sleep through stars, avert expensive exclusivity, segregated summits. Debunk protest marches – our voices not squeaking as they do.

There under the wooden desk where mould has started to grow, we'll find organic wind and kindness. Reach beyond the fillers to terra firma. Grind and bind, break and brake. We're tossed to electronic song, squeaking to the rudder of daily news blasts. But we can't be angry. I'll wrap my arms around you, crying nomad, nomad, nomad till we're one or this and that.

Pigeons

Among all the green trousers and rotten cell-eyes, she keeps a placid poise. Cute and comfortable, sitting cross-legged behind bars, chewing gum, nonchalant on cement. Her nightly dose of methadone makes her a child again – waiting for a late-night glass of milk. Hair in blonde braids. Fumbling through her paper bag of goodies. "Drug bust, heroin," she says. Uses toilet paper to plug an ear sore, talks my ear off. I'm stunned – I've got a buddy. We could've hung out in the yard together, singing like pigeons, I'm certain.

Beggars

How you make us wince, fear that crush. Make us keep a raging pace. Tire us by advising us there's never enough. How can we be improved? Before you we are hunched and slumped, retreating from our selves, all that was in place before we came. You show us just how much we can't, inform us of what we're missing, dwell in us as desperate as breath.

Talking to the Un-Dead on Facebook

Gone is the journey to Kafka, Tolstoy – we're morphed
and hiding in virtual time. There's no cottage saved from
YouTube deliria, vampire delights. Our digital brains rene-
gades for damage control, status updates, twitter feeds, warm
sweaters, and snow. There'll be a telepathic revolution – Star
Trek transporters avenging via wireless interfaces. Millions in
happy time – arriving nowhere. Screen face photos traced,
slave hungry users killing languages in silence. E-friendships
on sale – the jackpot a thousand-plus friends – the dead ones
living in profiles and timelines. It's all now. Instantaneous.
Becoming more and more dead. Beginning with post-
ings – shares to the un-dead. Buried in e-deeds. Live sé-
ances all e-bright, a-flicker. Hydra channel of virtual spoil.
Incognito is free exchange on a succubus screen-void-of-flesh.
Overstimulate one sense, deny another. The holy wire spouts
from the god-head electric. The weather-effect of wired iden-
tity, wireless words. The dead on screen our stardust.

When Lovers Wear Masks

It's a carnival act,
camouflage among the sheets.

Clothes donned
and dropped

the night before.
Chagrined perfumes,

aphrodisiac instants
stirring the stomach,

enticing the tongue.
Captured Casanova time –

a Ferris wheel
shadows its turning.

Thirst

Drinking ritual,
red jest,
deputy of the grail.

Glands and tongue
hydrating,
taste of grape.

Dipped in sweat,
adjacent to permission
and holy blood.

Us

I keep your metaphysic
in me larger than
your drab blanket,
favourite shoes,

choose to welcome anxiety –
we're attendant to the scalding
sounds of beating aorta,
twisted pulse,

slow and starry
remnants of meteor-memory.
The mixed message of atmosphere –
warm, then icy,

combustible,
sharing of she and he,
or just this rock –
that plastic recycled us.

We don't like it much.
But how to breathe
into our entrance and exits,
original tenderness.

Mother and Glenn Gould

On Saturday afternoons she lets him in. He enters coy, keys into keys. Does not remove his shoes. Flits through doors and cupboards, shelves. Pirouettes in the rooms of my youth, taking his lyrical leaps. One moment *pianissimo*, another *pianoforte*. Bach to Beethoven and back. Around her everything glows orange.

Exaltation in the Key of Quiet

I am not here to hear, to listen, to tell you
anything, only to accompany you
through silence.

Notes

"Pew" is for Wislawa Symborska.

"The Words" is for Susan Musgrave.

"Imaginings" is after Nicholas Power's poem "A Modest Device," *GesturePress Blog:* www.gesturepress.wordpress.com and references artist Paterson Ewen. "Just enough skin for this world" refers to the following lines in Power's poem: "imagine his playful work assumes the exact shape of your longing/ the artist constructing just enough skin/ between himself and the world."

"Pilgrim" is after Czeslaw Milosz, "If There is No God," *The New Yorker,* August 30, 2004.

"Ghost Dialogue" is after Elizabeth Smart, *By Grand Central Station I Sat Down and Wept.* (London: Grafton Books, 1966).

"The Hangman Favours Apollo" is after Sylvia Plath's poem "The Hanging Man" in *Sylvia Plath: Ariel. The Restored Edition. A Facsimile of Plath's Manuscript, Reinstating Her Original Selection and Arrangement.* (New York: Harper Collins, 2004).

"Skins Over Pompeii" is after Pat Lowther's poem "Skin Over Pompeii" in *The Collected Works of Pat Lowther: Later Uncollected and Unpublished Work 1968-1975.* Ed. Wiesenthal, Christine. (Edmonton: NewWest Press, 2010: 153).

"Soothsayer" is for Clara Blackwood.

"Blue Flowering" is after a visual piece by artist Holly Briesmaster titled "Blue Flowering, Acrylic On Fan."

"Death Fruit" is after Pier Paolo Pasolini's poems "Nineteen Forty-Four" and "Nineteen Forty-Five" in *Pasolini Between Enigma and Prophecy*. Zigaina, Giuseppe. Transl. Russell, Jennifer. (Toronto: Exile Editions, 1991).

"How I'd Like To Die" is after David W. McFadden's poem "How I'd Like to Die" in *The Art of Darkness*. (Toronto: McClelland and Stewart, 1984: 41).

Acknowledgements

I thank the editors and publishers of the following publications in which earlier versions of poems in this collection have appeared:

"The End of the Affair," "The Old World" in *Bravo! A Selection of Prose and Poetry by Italian Canadian Writers* (Quattro Books, 2012); "Zuppolone" in *Italians at Table: An Anthology of Food* (Guernica Editions, forthcoming); "Pompeii" in *Poem with Poet Profile* (*The Toronto Quarterly Blog*, April 2010); "Death Fruit" in *Poet to Poet* (Guernica Editions, 2012); "Now You Know," "The End of the Affair," "The Old World," "The Words" in *Rewriting Cities, Rewriting Self: An Anthology of Italian Canadian Poets in Toronto* (University of Toronto Press, 2012); "Aria for Evita" in *Vulva Magic: A Chapbook* (LyricalMyrical Press, 2004).

I would like to sincerely thank the following individuals for their unending support: Eva Marie Tropper, Julie Carrier, Rebecca Leonard, Rachel Brophy, Sarah Armenia, Antonietta Di Placido, Domenica Conte, Mary Chestnut, Gianna Patriarca, Bruna Di Giuseppe-Bertoni, Allan and Holly Briesmaster, Clara Blackwood, Shawn MacLeod, Carri Edwards, Luciano Iacobelli, John Calabro, Lisa Young, David Chilton, Susan Musgrave, Catherine Graham and Carol Barbour. I also want to emphasize the Canadian and international poets who have inspired many of the pieces in this book through the legacy of their work.

I thank the following associations and programs for their assistance in the development of my work over the past five years: The Association of Italian Canadian Writers, Quattro WordStage Reading Series, The Art Bar Poetry Series, Hot-Sauced Words, Stuart Ross Poetry Workshops, and the Plasticine Poetry Series.

Finally, a huge thank you to Elana Wolff for her edit of this collection, for being patient and believing in my process; publishers Michael Mirolla and Connie Guzzo-McParland for continuing to foster the growth of Guernica Editions as a literary press; and Guernica's founder and former publisher, Antonio D'Alfonso, whom I've watched work with unending devotion at this labour of love.

About The Book

Exaltation in Cadmium Red splatters and brushes in poems, both as a toxic, poisonous, metallic mix, and a rich, vibrant, powerful oil colour. Shades of cadmium red have persisted throughout history as the most exuberant in the oil-paint palette; the hues meant to be mixed with other oils in subtle, specific, and precise doses for greatest effect. This body of poems revels in this fanatical, fantastic colour to express the heights and depths of passion – engaging in meditations on prayer, spirituality, feminism, and the breadth of existence in a post-colonial, trans-national and transsexual age.

Praise for *Exaltation in Cadmium Red*

Sonia Di Placido's poems are eloquent and intelligent, free, dark and painfully beautiful. They are solitary planets of energy in their unique trajectory searching for and growing towards other powerful forces.

– Gianna Patriarca

The poems in Sonia Di Placido's *Exaltation in Cadmium Red* lay authoritative and stylish claim to an older, deeper, more poetically acute and powerful song than is often heard in Canadian poetry. They evoke ancient passion – passion in all its senses of fullness of erotic feeling, suffering, and spirituality; they seem drawn molten out of the fires of experience and out of the poet's vulnerable, desirous, fierce core at "absolute stations of [her] dance with words." At their most sensitively pitched and concentrated, these utterances pour themselves into phrasings of such inordinate evocativeness and beauty that they set forth imaginative apprehensions of a divine erotic reality. They're "dipped in sweat,/ adjacent to permission/ and holy blood." They move through "lush networks of/ fortune"; they "waltz/ in vineyards,/ drunk on audacity." They enact an exultant roving fire and burning – yet they live within "the bounds of ... aperture or design." This is the secret of the poet of *Exaltation in Cadmium Red:* Out of her "fierce respect for mystery" she creates intense poetic forms that are "subtle, sacred, and sleek" and that succeed in "releasing ... awe."

– Russell Thornton

About The Author

Sonia Di Placido is a writer, performer, and artist current-
ly completing the Creative Writing, Optional Residency
MFA Program, with the University of British Columbia.
She is also a graduate of the Ryerson University Theatre
School and holds an honours degree in Humanities from
York University. She has worked as a Supernumerary with
the Canadian Opera Company and is a member of the
Association of Italian Canadian Writers. Sonia has pub-
lished profile pieces, creative non-fiction, and poems in liter-
ary journals and anthologies.

POET TO POET: POEMS WRITTEN TO POETS
AND THE STORIES THAT INSPIRED THEM

The idea for Poet to Poet was sparked in fall of 2010 – at a Guernica launch in Toronto's Little Italy. A young author had closed her reading with a moving poem about another poet, prefaced by an anecdote on how the piece had come into being. The audience was engaged and the response was particularly enthusiastic. As I stepped up to the stage to close the set, I thought: What a collection that could be – a book of poems written to, for, about, or.... – *Elana Wolff*

BY AVAILABLE LIGHT

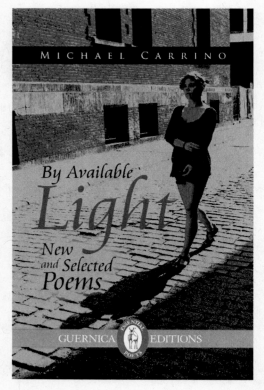

By Available Light is a book of poetry in which Michael Carrino offers poems from his four published books, along with a group of recent poems, to continue an exploration of how the act of reverie casts a sometimes pale, sometimes vivid light using evocative, sensual images of object, place, and person to remember, make sense of such remembering, and to effect how we make our way through a life.